Sally

Lehrwerk für den
Englischunterricht ab Klasse 3

Pupil's Book 4

Ausgabe Bayern

Erarbeitet von
Martina Bredenbröcker, Würzburg
Jasmin Brune, Sonsbeck
Daniela Elsner, Frankfurt/Main
Barbara Gleich, Uhingen
Stefanie Gleixner-Weyrauch, München
Simone Gutwerk, Würzburg
Marion Lugauer, Erding
Sabine Schwarz, Winsen/Luhe

Unter Beratung von
Jane Brockmann-Fairchild, Bidingen

Illustriert von
Barbara Jung, Wilfried Poll,
Anja Boretzki, Andreas Fischer, Renate Möller,
Thilo Pustlauk, Gisela Vogel

Oldenbourg Schulbuchverlag, München

Inhalt (★ Unit optional)

pupil's CD / teacher's CD

teacher's CD only

Sally's task

★ extra

Work with a partner.

Work in groups.

Think. Pair. Share.

Write.

Draw.

Speak.

Rap: Welcome back to school!

Step to the left, step to the right.

Raise your  and feel alright.

Turn around and say, "That's cool!"

Welcome back to school!

Sit on your , write in the air.

Let's have fun with English.

Dance to the beat and say, "That's cool!"

Welcome back to school!

Around the classroom you must look.

Put your  on the  .

Turn around and say, "That's cool!"

Welcome back to school!

1 Listen and sing.

2 Act out the rap.

Let's play a board game!

1 **Play in groups (2–5). Roll the dice. Take turns.**

Red number:
Do what it says or answer the question.
If you can't, miss a turn.

The winner is the first to reach finish.

If you don't know a word, look it up in your dictionary.
Name the days of the week.
Stand on 1 leg for 30 seconds.
What's your favourite toy?
Say a rhyme or sing a song.
What's your telephone number?
Name 5 things in your classroom.
Sing a birthday song.
Name 5 different kinds of fruit.
How do you feel today?
What's the weather like today?
Who is this?
Show me your socks. What colour are they?
What's the name of your best friend?
FINISH
MAY
5
39 40 41 42 43 44 45 46 47 48 49 50 51 52 53 54 55 56 57 58 59 60 61 62 63 64 65 66 67 68 69 70 71 72 73 74 75 76 77 78 79 80

What time is it?

1 **Listen and point.**

2 **Check the time and speak:**
What time is it? It's …

Set the clock. Ask your partner:
What time is it?

 CD 1.5

Gavin the ghost

1 Listen and read.

2 Act out the story.

At the hotel

1 **Look at the hotel. What's wrong? Tell your partner.**

The bed is too small.

The chair is too big.

Do you like my hotel / the room? –
Yes, I do. / No, I don't.
I like ... / I don't like ...
It has got ... /
It hasn't got ...
How much is it?
How many rooms have you got?

2 **Design your own special hotel. Show it to your partner. Talk about it.**

Think. Pair. Share.

I have a big/... hotel. This is my room. It's small./...

Write an ad for your hotel.

Presentation tips:
- Speak loudly and clearly.
- Look at the class.
- Show pictures.

chair table classroom teacher book
pen pencil rubber schoolbag picture

1 **Look and speak.**

2 **Where are your school things?**
My pencil is in/on … the …

in on under behind
in front of next to

Compare the words in English and German:
bathroom – Badezimmer, kitchen – Küche

- Ich kann auf Englisch nach der Uhrzeit fragen.
- Ich kann die Uhrzeit benennen.
- Ich kann einige Zimmer und Möbel benennen.
- Ich kann ein Klassenzimmer beschreiben.
- Ich kann sagen, wo etwas ist.
- Ich kann sagen, dass etwas zu groß oder zu klein ist.

Let's make Sally's sandwich!

Take a slice of bread.
Put it on a plate.

Spread butter and ketchup on it.

Cut the tomato, the egg and the cucumber.
Put them on the bread.

Put some ham, cheese and lettuce on it.

Put another slice of bread on top.

Cut the sandwich in half.
Sally's sandwich is ready to eat!

1 **Look and read.**

2  **Make your own sandwich:**
What do you want to put on your sandwich?
Make a shopping list in your group.
Talk about who wants to bring the bread, ham, …

It's lunchtime

Many people eat hamburgers at a diner.

You can find many fish and chips shops in England.

Create your own salad from the salad bar.

1 **Look and read.**

2 **Listen to the text. What do Emily and Phil order?**

3 **Where do you have lunch? What do you take to eat/drink? Act out the scene.**

I take … to eat.

I take … to drink.

Hobbies

riding a horse | riding a bike | playing the guitar
reading books | ice skating | playing the piano | snowboarding
playing tennis | playing football | swimming

1 **Look at the pictures.**
What are their hobbies?
Tim's hobby is … / Tim likes …

2 **Write a word web with hobby words.**
Use your dictionary.

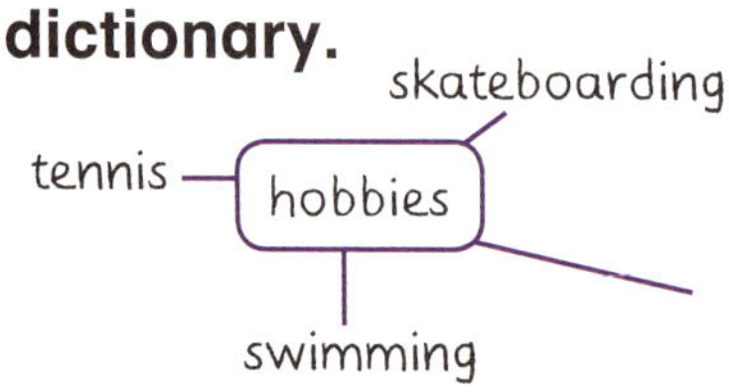

3 **What's your hobby?**
Show your photos and tell your class.
Use your dictionary. My hobby is … / I like …

The interview

1 **Ask your partner.**

Can you ...?

Yes, I can.

No, I can't.

Can you	play football/tennis
	sing a song
	play the guitar
	ride a skateboard
	inline skate

2 **Listen to the interview with Dirk Nowitzki.**

Dirk Nowitzki likes playing basketball.

3 **Do your own interview.**

Emily's day

At 8 o'clock I get up and have breakfast.

School begins at 9 o'clock.

At 12:30 I have lunch.

At 3 o'clock I go home.

At 3:45 I do my homework.

At 5 o'clock I call my friends and we play football.

At 6:15 I have dinner.

At 7 o'clock I read a book or watch TV.

At 8 o'clock I go to bed. Good night!

1 Listen, look and read.

2 What about your day? Tell your partner:

In the morning …
In the afternoon …
In the evening/At night …

And what do you do at the weekend? Talk to your partner.

MY WEEKEND
On Saturday, I get up at … /
On Sunday, I …

At the same time

Somewhere in the world school starts.
At the same time …

… a little cat
spills a glass of lemonade …

… a shark
looks for some food
in the ocean …

… a baby eats
some chocolate
ice cream …

… a skateboard
rolls down a hill …

… a father forgets
about his pancake …

… a mouse kisses
a horse …

… somewhere in the world school is over.

1 **Look and read.**

2  **What else happens at the same time? Talk to your class.**

3  **Make your own storybook. Use your dictionary.**

Checkpoint 2

1 **Look and speak.**

read books play football / tennis
ride a horse / bike / skateboard swim

2 **Write a word web with food and drink words. Use your dictionary.**

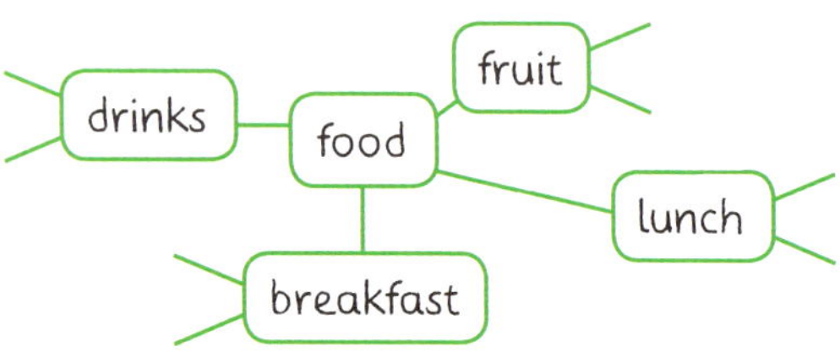

3 **Make a shopping list for a picnic.**
I need ...

a or **an? What's the rule?**
an apple, **an** egg, a plum, a football ...
Find more examples.

- Ich kann etwas zum Essen oder Trinken bestellen.
- Ich kann eine Einkaufsliste erstellen.
- Ich kann auf Englisch nach einem Hobby fragen.
- Ich kann sagen, was ich gerne tue.
- Ich kann jemanden fragen, ob er etwas kann.
- Ich kann sagen, was ich kann oder nicht kann.

In the supermarket

1 **Listen and point.**

2 **Make your own shopping list. Use your dictionary. Read, look up and write down.**

3 **Talk to your partner.**

Have you got chicken (ham, sweets ...) on your shopping list?

Yes, I have.

No, I haven't.

Something good

1 Listen to the story and point to the pictures.

2 Can you tell the story in German?

3 What can you buy in a supermarket?
In a supermarket I can buy…

 CD 1.25

went shopping with her father.

"My gets ."

Tyya put 100 boxes of into her cart.

"Daddy, look! Good food!"

"Oh, no! Put it all back!"

Tyya put back the 100 boxes of . She put 300 into her cart.

"Daddy, look! Good food!"

"Oh, no! Put it all back! Don't move."

Tyya didn't move. A lady came by and looked at Tyya.
The lady put a price tag on Tyya's .
She picked Tyya up and put her
on the shelf with all the other dolls.

A man came along and looked at Tyya.

"I'm going to get that for my son."

"STOP!"

Then Tyya's father came along.

"Tyya? Tyya? Where are you? What are you doing on that shelf?"

He gave Tyya a big kiss. Then they went to pay.

"Hey, Mister. You have to pay for her."

"This is my kid. I won't pay."

"Yes!"

"NO!"

Daddy paid the man. Tyya gave her father a big kiss.

"Daddy, you finally bought something good."

4 **Read the text. Practise in your group. Act it out.**

Jack and the beanstalk

1 **Listen, look and point.**

2 **Act out the story.**

 CD 1.27

Let's act it out!

Reading and learning the story

Painting the background

Making the music

Telling the story with shadow puppets

Practising the story

Performing the story

Transport in London

1 Look and read.

The red double-decker bus is famous in London.

The traditional London taxi is black. You drive on the left-hand side of the road.

The underground in London is one of the oldest in the world.

There are lots of ferries on the River Thames.

2 Look at the photos and read.

Compare to other cities. Where do you live?
What can you see in your town? Talk to your partner.

Detective Brighthead

1 **Listen to the story and look at the pictures.**

2 **Which vehicles does Mr Brighthead take? Read, look up and write down.** He takes the …

The clever tortoise

1 **Listen, look and read.**

The 5-minute zoo game

Play with a partner.

Play for 5 minutes.

Roll the dice.

Take turns.

The winner is the player who has got the most points.

Move in any direction.

Animal picture:
Name the animal = 1 point.
Name the animal and describe it = 2 points.

Snack stop: You must pay.
Miss a turn.

Crocodile: Bad luck!
You lose 1 point.

NY

dress pair of jeans pullover shirt
pair of shoes perfect too big/small

1 **Look and speak.**

2 **Which shops do you know? What can you buy there?**
At the toy shop I can buy ...

3 **Write a word web with animal words.**
Use your dictionary.

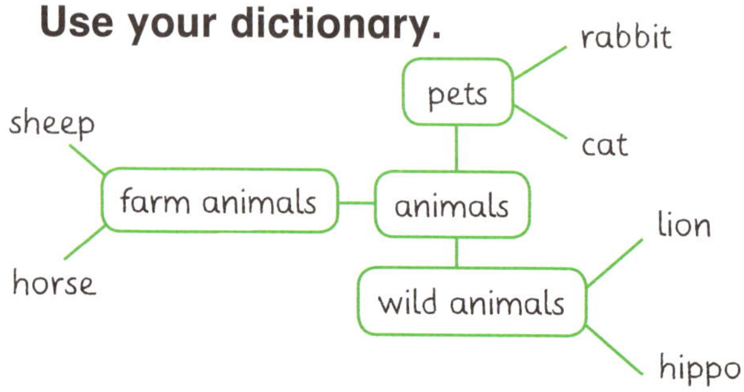

Find the plural. Use your dictionary.
-s: cat – cats **no -s:** sheep – sheep

fish horse mouse
dog goose hamster

- Ich kann verschiedene Geschäfte benennen.
- Ich kann ein Verkaufsgespräch in einem Geschäft führen.
- Ich kann auf Englisch einige Verkehrsmittel benennen.
- Ich kann erfragen, wie ich zu einem bestimmten Ort gelange.
- Ich kann verschiedene Tiere benennen.
- Ich kann ein Tier genauer beschreiben.

Sally and the Loch Ness Monster

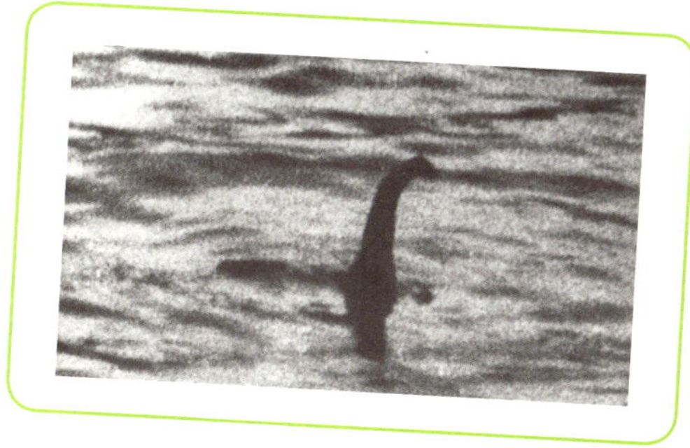

1 Listen, look and point.

2 Read and tell the story.

3 Draw your own Nessie. Describe her to your class.

A holiday trip to Scotland

1 **Look and speak:**
Mr Brown wants to see …

2 **Plan your own holiday trip to Scotland.**
Find out about Scotland on the Internet. I want to see …

Scottish dance

1 **Listen, sing and dance.**

A rainbow of friends

Some friends are funny.

Some friends are stars.

Some friends wear clothing that's different than ours.

But all friends are special.

We all have our interests.

We all have our strengths and weaknesses too.

If we work hand in hand, all jobs can be done.

If we play as a team, we've already won.

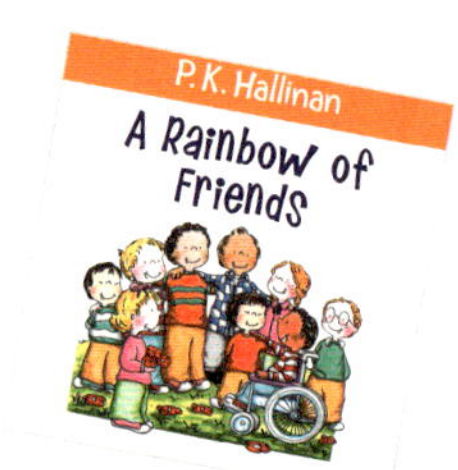

1 **Read the story and tell it in German.**

2 **What's special about your friends? Tell your class.**

3 **What are friends for? Talk in groups.**

We all live in the same world

Hola!

Juanita

Bonjour!

Jacqueline

Ciao!

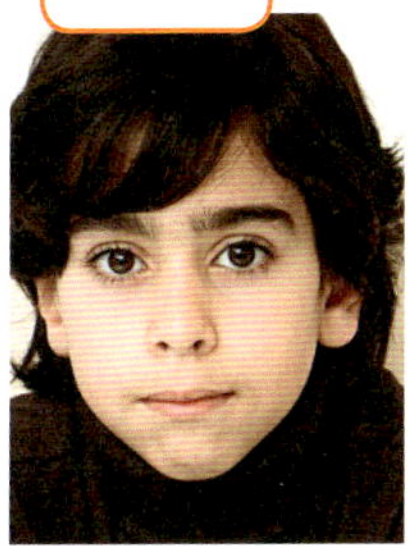

Paolo

Hello!

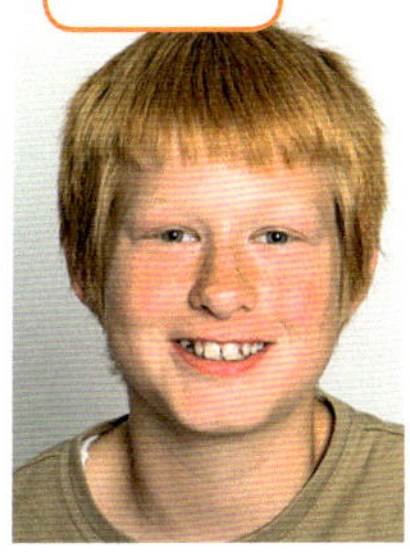

Thomas

Hallo!

Maria

Merhaba!

Güler

Jassu!

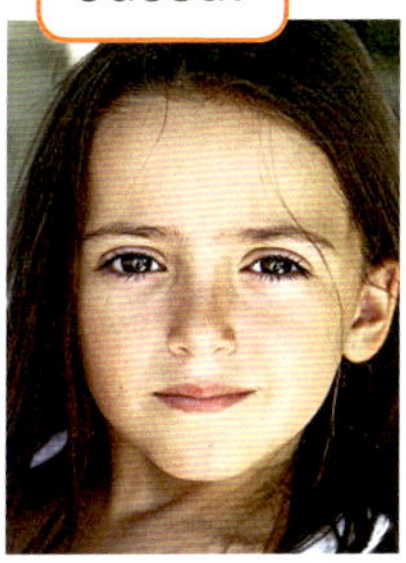

Dimitra

Priwjet!

Sergej

I'm from …	I speak …
England	English
France	French
Germany	German
Greece	Greek
Italy	Italian
Russia	Russian
Spain	Spanish
Turkey	Turkish

But we all laugh in the same language.
We all like to sing and play.
We all live in the same world,
no matter where we're from.

I'm from …

I speak …

1 **Listen and sing.**

2 **Where are you from? What language(s) do you speak? Talk to your partner.**

What's the word for Hello **in different languages? Make a list.**

This is me!

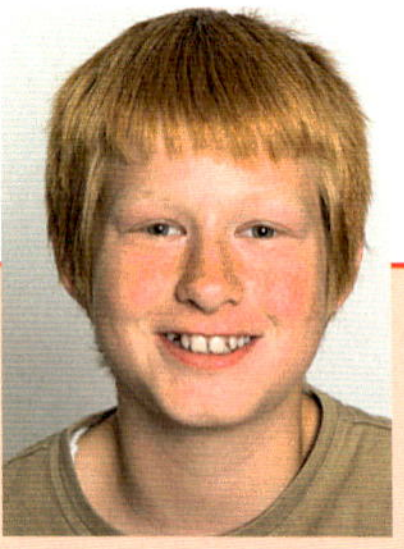

My name is Thomas.
I live in London.
I'm 9 years old.
I speak English and German.
I've got 2 sisters,
Mary and Liz.
I like playing football.
I want to be a teacher.
My favourite food is
chicken and chips and
chocolate ice cream.

My name is
Güler.
I'm from
Turkey.
I'm 10 years old.
I speak Turkish and English.
My hobbies are swimming
and riding a horse.
My favourite pet is a cat.

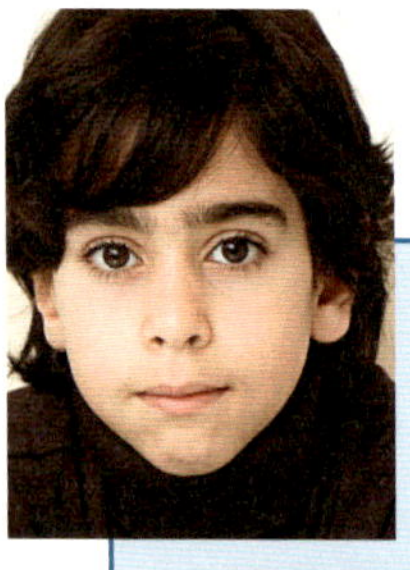

My name is Paolo.
I'm from Italy.
I'm 9 years old.
I speak Italian and English.
I've got a dog. His name is Rocco.
My brother Enrico is 11 years old,
my sister Stella is 7 years old.
I can play the piano.
I love pizza with ham and strawberries.

1 **Listen and read.**

2 **Write about yourself. Present your text to your class.**
My name is ... I live in ... I speak ...

England English German Germany
Russian Turkish teacher

1 **Look and speak.**

2 **Do an interview with the captain. Act it out with your partner.**
What's your name? / Where are you from? / When's your birthday? / How old are you? / …

3 **Write about yourself. Use your dictionary.** My name is ... I'm ...

Compare the words in English and German: Italy – Italien, Spain – Spanien

- ✓ Ich kann etwas über Schottland erzählen.
- ✓ Ich kann jemanden auf Englisch nach seinem Beruf fragen.
- ✓ Ich kann sagen, was ich werden will.
- ✓ Ich kann sagen, aus welchem Land ich komme.
- ✓ Ich kann sagen, welche Sprache(n) ich spreche.
- ✓ Ich kann andere fragen, woher sie kommen und welche Sprache(n) sie sprechen.

Guy Fawkes Day – Bonfire Night

Penny for the Guy!

fireworks at night

bonfire at night

Remember, remember,
the 5th of November,
gunpowder, treason and plot.
I see no reason
why gunpowder treason
should ever be forgot.

Do you know why people celebrate Guy Fawkes Day?

1 Look at the photos. Read the text.

2 Listen to the story about Guy Fawkes.

Do you know other festivals with fireworks or bonfires?

Thanksgiving today

Mum gets up at 6 o'clock in the morning.
She puts the turkey into the oven.
The turkey takes 5 hours to cook.

At 12 o'clock my family comes to our house. We have our Thanksgiving dinner: turkey with potatoes, carrots, corncobs and pumpkin pie.

In the afternoon we go to the Thanksgiving parade.

In the evening we watch the football match on TV.

1 **Listen to the story of Carol's Thanksgiving.**

2 **Look at the photos and read.**

3 **Write a Thanksgiving invitation.**

A story about the first Thanksgiving

1 **Listen to the story about the first Thanksgiving.**

2 **Look at the picture. What can you see?**

pumpkin corncobs potatoes tomatoes
beans turkey Indians settlers fishing

3 **What do you know about the American Indians?**

CD 2.25

Come to the USA!

A cowboy in Texas shows how he works.

The Mississippi is a very long river.
You can take a ride on a steamboat.

The Grand Canyon National Park is in Arizona. The views are great!

The Statue of Liberty is in New York.

The President of the USA lives in the White House in Washington, D.C.

In San Francisco, California, cable cars go up and down the roads.

1 **Look at the photos.**

2  **What do you know about the USA?**

3  **Make a poster, a collage or a report about the USA. Present it to your class.**

In the USA you pay with dollars ($).

Father Christmas in Australia

1. Listen and point.
2. Act out the story.
3. How do you celebrate Christmas in your family?
4. Write a Christmas card.

The 5 days of Christmas

kookaburra

On the first day of Christmas
my true love sent to me
a  in a gum tree.

On the second day of Christmas
my true love sent to me
2 small 
and a  in a gum tree.

koala

cockatoo

On the third day of Christmas
my true love sent to me
3 ,
2 small …

On the fourth day of Christmas
my true love sent to me
4 ,
3 …

crocodile

kangaroo

On the fifth day of Christmas
my true love sent to me
5 ,
4 …

1 **Look at the photos. Listen and sing.**

2 **Write word cards for a Christmas bingo. Read, look up and write down.** sleigh, reindeer, stocking, present, star, Christmas tree, winter, cold, snowy…

Let's go to Australia!

Sydney is the biggest city.

A road train is a very long truck.

Ayers Rock is a big flat rock.

At the Great Barrier Reef you can see corals and coloured fish.

An Australian Aborigine is playing the didgeridoo.

1 **Look at the photos.**

2 **Listen and point.**

3 **Read the text. Find the correct photo.**

Look and draw your own traffic sign.

Let's make an Easter bunny mosaic card!

You need:
coloured eggshells
cardboard
a pencil
glue
scissors

Funny little bunny
goes hop, hop, hop!
Funny little bunny,
please stop, stop, stop!

Break the eggshells into small pieces.

Draw your Easter bunny on the cardboard. Cut it out.

Glue the eggshells on your Easter bunny.

Glue your Easter bunny onto the cardboard. Write an Easter greeting on your card.

1 **Look and read. Make your own Easter card. Write "Happy Easter!" on your card.**

2 **Can you say "Happy Easter!" in other languages?**

Hi Noah,
Greetings from .
I'm having a great weekend at the beach.
I see lots of sheep and kiwis.
Yours,
Henry

Dear Sarah,
Greetings from .
I'm on a safari with my family.
I'm taking lots of pictures of elephants and zebras.
It's great!
Yours,
Anne

1 ✎ **In which countries do people speak English? Make a list.**

2 **Read the postcards. Where are they from?**

3 ✎ **Write your own postcard.**
Hello ... I'm ... I like ... It's ... Yours ...

Words

Back to school
Zurück in der Schule

eleven elf
twelve zwölf
thirteen dreizehn
fourteen vierzehn
fifteen fünfzehn
sixteen sechzehn
seventeen siebzehn
eighteen achtzehn
nineteen neunzehn
twenty zwanzig
thirty dreißig
forty vierzig
fifty fünfzig
sixty sechzig
seventy siebzig
eighty achtzig
ninety neunzig
a/one hundred hundert

clock Uhr
hand (Uhr-)Zeiger
(to) set stellen

What time is it? Wie spät ist es?

It's 1 (2, 3 ...) o'clock.
Es ist 1 (2, 3 ...) Uhr.

It's **1 (2, 3 ...):15.**
Es ist 1 (2, 3 ...):15.

It's **1 (2, 3...):30.**
Es ist 1 (2, 3 ...):30.

It's **1 (2, 3 ...):45.**
Es ist 1 (2, 3 ...):45.

At home Zu Hause

attic Speicher
bathroom Badezimmer
bedroom Schlafzimmer
castle Schloss, Burg
cellar Keller
garden Garten
hiccups Schluckauf
kitchen Küche
living room Wohnzimmer
stairs Treppen
toilet Toilette, WC

bed Bett
chair Stuhl
furniture Möbel
just right genau richtig
lamp Lampe
room Zimmer
shelves Regal
sofa Sofa
table Tisch
too big zu groß
too small zu klein
wardrobe Schrank

Where is ...? – He/She/It is in the ...
Wo ist ...? – Er/Sie/Es ist im/in der ...

Is he/she/it in the ...? –
Yes, he/she/it is. / No, he/she/it isn't.
Ist er/sie/es im/in der ...? – Ja. / Nein.

Let's have lunch
Lass(t) uns Mittag essen

bread Brot
butter Butter
cheese Käse

chicken and chips Hühnchen mit Pommes frites
cucumber Gurke
egg Ei
fish and chips Fisch mit Pommes frites
ham Schinken
hamburger Hamburger
hot dog Hotdog
ketchup Ketchup
lettuce Kopfsalat
lunch Mittagessen
pizza Pizza
salad Salat
sandwich Sandwich
sausage with mashed potatoes Würstchen mit Kartoffelbrei
soup Suppe
spaghetti Spaghetti
to take nehmen
tomato Tomate

cup Tasse
fork Gabel
glass Glas
knife – knives Messer – Messer (Plural)
plate Teller
spoon Löffel

Can I help you? – Yes. I'd like ..., please.
Kann ich dir/euch/Ihnen helfen? – Ja. Ich hätte gerne ..., bitte.

Would you like something to drink? – Yes, please. I'd like a glass of ..., please.
Hättest du / Hätten Sie gerne etwas zu trinken? – Ja, bitte. Ich hätte gerne ein Glas ..., bitte.

I take ... to eat/drink.
Ich nehme ... zum Essen/Trinken.

How much is it? –That's ... pounds.
Wieviel macht/kostet das? – Das macht/kostet ... Pfund.

Here you are. Hier, bitte.

Hobbies and sports
Hobbys und Sportarten

basketball Basketball
book Buch
(to) do tun, machen
fun Spaß
great großartig
hobby – hobbies Hobby – Hobbys
ice skating Schlittschuhfahren
interview Interview
(to) love sehr gerne mögen, lieben
okay in Ordnung, OK
(to) play football Fußball spielen
(to) play the piano/the guitar Klavier/Gitarre spielen
(to) read lesen
reporter Reporter
(to) ride a horse ein Pferd reiten
(to) ride a bike Fahrrad fahren
(to) run rennen, laufen
snowboarding Snowboarden
sports Sport(arten)
sports star Sportstar
(to) swim schwimmen
tennis Tennis

What's your hobby? – My hobby is ... / I like ... Was ist dein Hobby? – Mein Hobby ist ... / Ich mag gerne ...

Words

Do you like ...? – Yes, I do. / No, I don't. Magst du ...? – Ja. / Nein.

Can you play ...? – Yes, I can. / No, I can't. Kannst du ... spielen? – Ja. / Nein.

My day Mein Tagesablauf

morning Morgen, Vormittag
afternoon Nachmittag
evening Abend
night Nacht

at the same time zur selben Zeit
breakfast Frühstück
(to) brush bürsten
(to) call rufen, anrufen
dinner Abendessen
(to) get up aufstehen
(to) go to bed zu Bett gehen
(to) go to school zur Schule gehen
(to) learn lernen
lunch Mittagessen
(to) play spielen
time Zeit
(to) watch TV fernsehen

What do you do at ... o'clock? Was machst du (normalerweise) um ... Uhr?

I do my homework. Ich mache meine Hausaufgaben.

Shopping Einkaufen

apple Apfel
biscuit Keks
cheese Käse
cherry Kirsche
chocolate Schokolade
chocolate bar Schokoriegel
egg Ei
fruit Frucht, Obst
ham Schinken
honey Honig
ice cream Eis(krem)
lemonade Limonade
milk Milch
orange Orange
orange juice Orangensaft
pear Birne
plum Pflaume
spinach Spinat
strawberry Erdbeere
sweets Süßigkeiten
vegetables Gemüse

book shop Buchladen
clothes shop Kleiderladen
computer shop Computerladen
music shop Musikgeschäft
restaurant Restaurant
shelf – shelves Regalbrett – Regal
shoe shop Schuhgeschäft
shop assistant Verkäufer(in)
shop Geschäft, Laden
shopping list Einkaufsliste
sports shop Sportgeschäft
supermarket Supermarkt
sweets shop Süßwarenladen
toy shop Spielwarenladen

Have you got ... on your shopping list? Hast du ... auf deiner Einkaufsliste?

In the supermarket (book shop ...) I can buy ... Im Supermarkt (Buchladen ...) kann ich ... kaufen.

Excuse me, please. Where can I buy ...? – Go to ... It's on the ... floor.
Entschuldigen Sie, bitte. Wo kann ich ... kaufen? – Gehe / Gehen Sie zu ... Das ist im ... Stock.

Jack and the beanstalk
Jack und die Bohnenranke

apple pie Apfelkuchen
beanstalk Bohnenranke
blood Blut
castle Schloss, Burg
(to) climb (up/down) (hinauf/hinab)klettern
Englishman Engländer
fairy tale Märchen
giant Riese
(to) grow wachsen
(to) live leben
magic bean Zauberbohne
new neu
(to) sell verkaufen
(to) smell riechen

Yummy! Lecker!

Transport Verkehrsmittel

boarding pass Bordkarte
car Auto
clockmaker Uhrmacher
detective Detektiv
(double-decker) bus (Doppeldecker-)Bus
(to) drive fahren
famous berühmt
ferry Fähre
left-hand traffic Linksverkehr
map Landkarte, Stadtplan
museum Museum
old – oldest alt – älteste(r, s)
plane Flugzeug
station Bahnhof, U-Bahn Station / U-Bahn Haltestelle
taxi Taxi
thief Dieb
train Zug
underground U-Bahn

How can I get from … to ...?
Wie kann ich von ... nach ... gelangen?

You can take the …
Du kannst / Sie können den (die, das) ... nehmen.

Let's take the …
Lass(t) uns den (die, das) ... nehmen.

I'm sorry! Es tut mir leid!

Wild animals Wildtiere

big groß
clever schlau
(to) climb klettern
dangerous gefährlich
elephant Elefant
fast schnell
fat dick, fett
(to) fly fliegen
funny komisch, lustig
giraffe Giraffe
hippo Nilpferd
jungle Dschungel
lion Löwe
long lang

Words

monkey Affe
(to) run rennen, laufen
snake Schlange
strong stark
tail Schwanz
tall groß, hoch
tortoise (Land-)Schildkröte
trunk Rüssel
wings Flügel
zebra Zebra
zoo Zoo

(to) chew kauen
(to) pull ziehen
rope Seil, Strick
tug-of-war Tauziehen

Guess my animal: It's … /
It has got … / It can … / It lives in …
Errate mein Tier: Es ist … /
Es hat … / Es kann … /
Es lebt in/im …

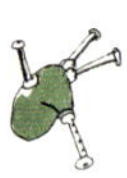

Going to Scotland
Nach Schottland reisen

castle Schloss, Burg
(to) go fishing zum Angeln gehen
Highland Games Highland Games
lake (der) See
Loch Ness Loch Ness
mountain Berg
Nessie Nessie
(to) plan a trip eine Reise planen
river Fluss
Scotland Schottland
sea Meer, (die) See
(to) take a photo ein Foto machen
(to) wait warten

I/We want to go to … Ich will /
Wir wollen nach … fahren.

I'd/We'd like to see …
Ich würde / Wir würden gerne …
sehen.

There's a … / There are …
Dort gibt es (ein, eine, einen) …

On Friday (Saturday …) we go to …
Am Freitag (Samstag …) fahren wir
nach …

On Friday (Saturday …) we visit …
Am Freitag (Samstag …) besichtigen
wir …

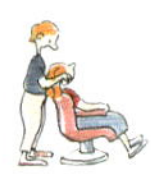

Jobs Berufe

(to) do tun, machen
(to) do my homework
meine Hausaufgaben machen
doctor Arzt, Doktor
(to) feed the cat die Katze füttern
hairdresser Friseur
(to) help in the house/kitchen/…
im Haus / in der Küche / … helfen
job Beruf, Aufgabe
(to) make my bed
mein Bett machen
policeman Polizist
policewoman Polizistin
room Zimmer
shop assistant Verkäufer(in)
teacher Lehrer(in)
(to) tidy my room
mein Zimmer aufräumen
(to) walk the dog
den Hund ausführen
(to) work arbeiten

What do you want to be? –
I want to be a ...
Was möchtest du werden? –
Ich möchte ... werden.

I have to ... Ich muss ...

Meeting people
Menschen begegnen

different verschieden, anders
friend Freund, Freundin
funny komisch, lustig
rainbow Regenbogen
special besonders
strength Stärke
weakness Schwäche

England England
English englisch
France Frankreich
French französisch
German deutsch
Germany Deutschland
Greece Griechenland
Greek griechisch
Italian italienisch
Italy Italien
language Sprache
Russia Russland
Russian russisch
Spain Spanien
Spanish spanisch
Turkey Türkei
Turkish türkisch
world Welt

Where are you from? – I'm from England (Germany ...).
Woher kommst du? – Ich komme aus England (Deutschland ...).

Are you from ...?
Kommst du aus ...?

Do you speak English (German ...)?
Sprichst du Englisch (Deutsch ...)?

What languages do you speak? –
I speak ...
Welche Sprachen sprichst du? –
Ich spreche ...

Guy Fawkes in Great Britain
Guy Fawkes in Großbritannien

bonfire Lagerfeuer, Freudenfeuer
fireworks Feuerwerk
Guy Fawkes Day Jahrestag der Guy-Fawkes-Verschwörung (5. November)

Thanksgiving in the USA
Erntedankfest in den USA

apple Apfel
bean Bohne
carrot Karotte, Möhre
corn(cob) Mais(kolben)
dollar **($)** Dollar
fruit Obst, Frucht
Indian Indianer, indianisch
pear Birne
pie Kuchen
plum Pflaume
potato – potatoes
Kartoffel – Kartoffeln
pumpkin Kürbis
ship Schiff
Thanksgiving Day Erntedankfest
Thanksgiving dinner Erntedank-Essen

Words

tomato – tomatoes
Tomate – Tomaten
turkey Truthahn
vegetables Gemüse

It's Thanksgiving Day.
Es ist Erntedankfest.

I'm thankful for ...
Ich bin dankbar für ...

Christmas in Australia
Weihnachten in Australien

first erste(r, s)
second zweite(r, s)
third dritte(r, s)
fourth vierte(r, s)
fifth fünfte(r, s)

Aborigine australischer Ureinwohner
capital Hauptstadt
city Stadt
cockatoo Kakadu
coral Koralle
crocodile Krokodil
didgeridoo Didgeridoo
kangaroo Känguru
koala Koala
kookaburra Kookaburra
(to) pull ziehen
reindeer Rentier(e)
road train Lastwagen
rock Fels
sleigh Schlitten

Merry Christmas!
Frohe Weihnachten!

Easter Ostern

(to) break zerbrechen
cardboard Tonpapier, Pappe
daffodil Narzisse, Osterglocke
Easter bunny Osterhase
egg Ei
eggshell Eierschale
fireside Kamin
flower Blume
hill Hügel
mountain Berg

Happy Easter! Frohe Ostern!

Der verbindliche Wortschatz ist **fett** gedruckt.

Important words (class 3 and 4)

A a
a/an ein, eine
about über, von
(I) am ich bin
and und
apple Apfel
(you) are (du) bist
at an, bei, in, um

B b
(to) be sein
behind hinter
big groß
bike Fahrrad
birthday Geburtstag
black schwarz
(black)board Tafel
blue blau
book Buch
boy Junge, Bub
bread Brot
brother Bruder
brown braun
butter Butter
bye auf Wiedersehen

C c
can/can't können/nicht können
cat Katze
chair Stuhl
cheese Käse
chicken Huhn, Hähnchen
chips Pommes frites
chocolate Schokolade
class Klasse
classroom Klassenzimmer
cold kalt
colour Farbe
(to) come kommen

D d
dear liebe(s, r)
(to) do tun
don't nicht tun
dog Hund
dress Kleid
drink/(to) drink Getränk/trinken

E e
(to) eat essen
egg Ei
England England
English englisch

F f
family Familie
father Vater
fine gut, schön
fish Fisch, Fische
football Fußball
friend Freund, Freundin
from von, aus
fruit Frucht, Obst

G g
German deutsch
Germany Deutschland
girl Mädchen
(to) give geben
(to) go gehen, fahren
good gut
great groß, großartig
green grün
grey grau

H h
Halloween Halloween
ham Schinken
hamster Hamster
happy glücklich
(to) have (got) haben
has (got) hat
haven't (got) nicht haben
he er
hello hallo
(to) help helfen
her ihr
here hier
his sein
hobby Hobby
horse Pferd
hot heiß
house Haus
how wie

I i
I ich
I'd ich würde
I'm ich bin
I've ich habe
in in
in front of vor
(he) is (er) ist
it es
its sein, ihr

Words

J j

jeans Jeans

K k

(to) know wissen, kennen

L l

(to) like mögen
little klein

M m

many viele
Merry Christmas! Frohe Weihnachten!
morning Morgen
mother Mutter
mouse Maus
much viel
my mein

N n

name Name
next to neben
no nein
not nicht

O o

o'clock Uhr
okay/OK gut
old alt
on auf
orange Orange/orange

P p

party Party
pen Füller
pencil Bleistift
pet Haustier
picture Bild
pink rosa, pink
(to) play spielen
please bitte
plum Pflaume
pullover Pullover
(to) put setzen, stellen, legen

R r

rabbit Kaninchen
red rot
(to) ride reiten, fahren
room Raum, Zimmer
rubber Radiergummi

S s

sad traurig
salad Salat
school Schule
schoolbag Schultasche
she sie
shirt Hemd
shoes Schuhe
sister Schwester
skateboard Skateboard
small klein
snowboard Snowboard
(I'm) sorry es tut mir leid
sports Sport(arten)
strawberry Erdbeere
sweets Süßigkeiten
(to) swim schwimmen

T t

(to) take nehmen
tea Tee
teacher Lehrer, Lehrerin
tennis Tennis
thank you/thanks danke
the der, die, das
there da, dort
they sie
this dies, diese(r, s)
time Zeit
to zu, nach, bis
tomato Tomate

U u

under unter

V v

very sehr

W w

water Wasser
we wir
weekend Wochenende
welcome willkommen
what was
when wann
where wo
white weiß
who wer

Y y

yellow gelb
yes ja
you du, ihr, Sie
your dein, euer, Ihr

Die Liste enthält den verbindlichen Wortschatz aus Klasse 3 und 4.